Len Chimbley's
dream
Questions and answers about God

Published by Redemptorist Publications
Alphonsus House Chawton Hants GU34 3HQ
www.shineonline.net

First printed 1989
Revised edition January 2003

Printed by Polar Group
ISBN 0 852231 115 X

CONTENTS

Part One

The old man with the long, white beard; the limitations of human language; creation and the Big Bang; the God who can't step in.

LEN
Er…excuse me.

GOD
Yes?

LEN
Am I right in thinking you are…er…God?

GOD
That is correct.

LEN
Can I introduce myself? I'm Len Chimbley.

GOD
I know.

LEN
Yes, of course you do. Silly of me. Anyway, Lord, I'm very pleased to meet you.

GOD
And I'm very pleased to meet you, Len.

LEN
The funny thing is, I recognised you immediately.

GOD
Does that surprise you?

LEN
It does a bit.

GOD
Why?

LEN
Well, I'd always *thought* of you as an old man with a long white beard sitting on a cloud, but I didn't think you'd *really* be like that.

GOD
What did you think I'd be like?

LEN
I don't know – but everyone keeps saying you're *not* an old man with a long white beard sitting on a cloud.

GOD
And here I am, an old man with a long white beard…

LEN
…sitting on a cloud. It's amazing. I was right all along.

GOD
Sorry to disappoint you, Len.

LEN
What do you mean?

GOD
The truth is, you were *not* right all along.

LEN
You mean, you're not an old man with a long white beard sitting on a cloud?

GOD
Of course not. How could I be?

LEN
But there you are in front of me.

GOD
Granted. But this is *your* dream, Len, not mine.

LEN
Oh, so I'm only *dreaming* you're an old man with a long white beard?

GOD
Correct.

LEN
So when I wake up I'll have to *stop* thinking of you as an old man with a long white beard sitting on a cloud?

GOD
Not if you don't want to.

LEN
What do you mean?

GOD
I mean it's fine by me if you think of me like that.

LEN
But you've just said you're *not* like that.

GOD
True, I'm not. But it's all right by me if you picture me like that.

LEN
But it's a false picture.

GOD
Oh yes.

LEN
Then why is it all right by you if I have that picture?

GOD
Because *any* picture you have of me will be false, so the crazier your picture is, the less likely you are to be taken in by it.

LEN
And my picture of you is crazy?

GOD
Absolutely crazy.

LEN
Oh.

GOD
But still fine by me.

LEN
So I can still think of you as an old man with a long white beard sitting on a cloud?

GOD
Of course. As long as you remember that I'm *not* old, I'm *not* a man, I *haven't* got a long white beard, and I *don't* sit on a cloud.

LEN
I see. Does that mean I can go on talking to you now?

GOD
As much as you like. Pull up a cloud and sit down.

LEN
Thanks.

GOD
Comfy?

LEN
Yes, thanks.

GOD
Good.

LEN
Er…It's been nice again, hasn't it?

GOD
Yes, it has. But is that all you want to talk about, the weather?

LEN
No. I've got lots I want to talk about. But I must admit I do feel a bit nervous.

GOD
Why?

LEN
Well, you are God: the almighty, the all-powerful creator of the universe.

GOD
And that makes you nervous?

LEN
Of course it does. It would make anybody nervous.

GOD
What are you nervous about?

LEN
I'm scared of saying the wrong thing, or not being reverent enough.

GOD
I shouldn't worry about that. I already know your thoughts so there is no point in hiding them, is there?

LEN
I suppose not. But there are lots of questions I want to ask – questions about you. And it just seems a bit impertinent.

GOD
What does?

LEN
Asking you questions at all.

GOD
Why? What's wrong with asking questions?

LEN
It makes it look as though I have doubts about you.

GOD
Does it?

LEN
Well, doesn't it?

GOD
Not as far as I'm concerned.

LEN
You mean, you don't mind me asking questions?

GOD
Not in the least. Why should I? Every question leads to me in the end.

LEN

So asking questions doesn't mean my faith is weak?

GOD

Quite the opposite. Believing anything and everything is the enemy of faith, not genuine searching.

LEN

Wow! This is wonderful. Now I'll be able to get the answers to all the questions I ever wanted to ask.

GOD

Sorry to disappoint you, Len, but I don't think you will.

LEN

But you just said you don't mind my asking questions.

GOD

I don't. You can ask as many as you like. It's just that you may not get the answers.

LEN

What, you'll *refuse* to answer me?

GOD

No, of course not. I'll do my very best to answer you. But you must realise that the answers I give may not be very satisfactory.

LEN

But that's absurd.

GOD

Why?

LEN

Because if you're God, you should know the answers to all my questions.

GOD

I didn't say I don't know the answers to your questions. I said I may not be able to give *you* a satisfactory answer.

LEN

Why ever not?

GOD
Think about it like this. Supposing dogs could communicate with one another. What would they "talk" about?

LEN
Oh, I don't know, er…food, bones, smells, chasing cats, lamp-posts…that sort of thing.

GOD
In other words, they'd "talk" about things within their experience?

LEN
I imagine so, yes.

GOD
And that would be limited to what dogs understand. Right?

LEN
Right.

GOD
Now, supposing you could speak doggy language. How easy do you think it would be to explain to your dog what you are doing when you are reading the newspaper?

LEN
Just using doggy language?

GOD
Just using doggy language.

LEN
Not very easy at all, I should think.

GOD
Why?

LEN
Because reading doesn't enter into a dog's experience, does it? Doggy language wouldn't be able to cope with the concept of reading.

GOD
So, trying to explain to your dog what you were doing when you were reading the newspaper would be an impossible task?

LEN
I suppose it would be.

GOD
Well, now do you understand why I might have difficulty in answering *your* questions about *me*?

LEN
You mean, human language can't cope with divine things?

GOD
Let's put it this way: it can't cope adequately.

LEN
But it's not totally useless?

GOD
Not totally. If it were totally useless there'd be no point in you asking me any questions at all. But if you ask questions you've always got to remember that your questions are limited by what you can understand; and my answers have to be limited by what

you can understand. It's not help if I give you answers you can't understand, is it?

LEN
That's true. So where do we go from here?

GOD
Why don't you just start asking me some questions and we'll see how it works out?

LEN
That sounds like a good idea.

GOD
Thanks, Len. Off you go, then. What's your first question?

LEN
Let's see. I think I'd like to begin by asking about the creation of the universe.

GOD
Starting with the easy ones, eh? All right, what do you want to know?

LEN
When did you create the universe?

GOD
You talk as though creation was a past event.

LEN
Well, science says the Big Bang happened millions of years ago.

GOD
And you think the Big Bang marked the beginning of creation?

LEN
It seems reasonable.

GOD
And what happened then?

LEN
Then you left the universe to evolve.

GOD
Left it?

LEN
I don't mean you went away. I mean you were there watching over it; but all the same, it evolved.

GOD
So the Big Bang was a bit like a child setting a spinning-top going on a table and then keeping an eye on it to make sure it didn't go over the edge?

LEN
That's a very good way of putting it.

GOD
So your idea is this: I created the universe a long, long time ago. And then I stood by and watched it evolving.

LEN
That's it. And if anything is going seriously wrong you can step in and put it right.

GOD
Some people would say an awful lot *is* going wrong – especially in this world. So why do you think I don't step in?

LEN
To be honest, that is a question that had occurred to me. But I didn't want to put you on the spot.

GOD
That's very considerate of you. But I don't mind being put on the spot. So, why do you think I don't step in?

LEN
I honestly don't know. It's a great mystery to me.

GOD
Does it ever occur to you that I don't step in because I *can't* step in?

LEN
Can't step in? But I thought you were all-powerful.

GOD
I am. But think for a moment. There's a very simple reason why I can't step in.

LEN
Sorry, you've got me stumped.

GOD
I can't step in because I'm already in.

LEN
Already in?

GOD
As much as I can be.

LEN
But I always thought you were totally separate from the universe, on a different plane of existence altogether.

GOD
I am on a totally different plane of existence; but that doesn't mean I'm totally separate from the universe.

LEN
I don't understand. It seems like a contradiction.

GOD
All right, let me try to explain. Imagine standing at the edge of a pool looking down at the reflections in it. You can see a reflection of the sky, and of trees along the side of the pool, and foliage along the banks. Now: could you have the reflections without the pool?

LEN
No, of course not.

GOD
Why not?

LEN
Because reflections need something to be reflected *in*.

GOD
So the reflections and the pool go together?

LEN
Yes.

GOD
But would you say the pool and the reflections are exactly the same kind of reality?

LEN
No. The pool is real, but the reflections are … well, reflections.

GOD
What's the difference?

LEN
Well, you can put your hand in the pool, but you can't touch a reflection, can you?

GOD
Exactly. And although you can't have reflections without the pool, you *can* have the pool without the reflections.

LEN
But surely there are *always* reflections in a pool?

GOD
Not necessarily. On a dark, overcast night you'd know the pool was there if you fell into it, but you wouldn't see any reflections.

LEN
True enough.

GOD
Now, the point I want to make is this: my relationship to the universe is a *little* bit like the relationship of the pool to the reflections. Just as the reflections cannot exist without the pool, so the universe cannot exist without me. In other words, wherever you see a reflection there must be a pool, and wherever you see a part of the universe there must be me.

LEN
Ah, I'm beginning to see what you're getting at now. Is that what we mean when we say, "God is everywhere"?

GOD
It is indeed, Len. But we haven't finished yet. So far I've given you a picture of how I'm in the universe; I permeate it through and through – as a pool permeates the reflections. But I'm also *distinct* from the universe. Can you see how?

LEN
I think so. Just as the pool is a distinct kind of reality, a higher kind of reality than the reflections, so you are distinct from the universe. Is that right?

GOD
It is. And do you see what that means?

LEN
It must mean that the universe depends on you.

GOD
Exactly. If I walked away from the universe the effect would be the same as a pool drying up. No pool, no reflections; no me, no universe.

LEN
So, the universe depends on you at every moment?

GOD
It does.

LEN
It depends on you right now, in fact?

GOD
Yes.

LEN
Even this dream I'm having depends on you?

GOD
Of course.

LEN
So, when we talk about your act of creation it would be more accurate to think of it not as something you once did long ago, but something you are doing right now?

GOD
Yes, it would.

LEN
It seems as though that idea I had about the Big Bang being your act of creation and then you leaving the universe to evolve on its own is pretty wide of the mark.

GOD
Well, what do you think?

LEN
I think I'll have to start thinking about creation in a very different way.

FOR THOUGHT AND DISCUSSION

- Is God a man?
- Can we have an accurate picture of what God is like in himself?
- Is human language useless for talking about God?
- Is creation an event in the past?
- If the Big Bang theory were conclusively proved to be true, how would it affect our idea of God?
- Where is God?
- Is God the same as the universe?
- How would you reply to someone who said, "No astronaut has ever seen God"?

Part Two

A picture of creation; divine manifestations; science and religion; the hidden God.

LEN
There's something puzzling me.

GOD
What's that?

LEN
It's to do with the example you gave of the pool and the reflections.

GOD
What's the problem?

LEN
Well, a pool can't help having reflections in it, can it? I mean, it doesn't *choose* to have reflections in it. It doesn't *create* the reflections. But you do create the universe.

GOD
You're absolutely right, Len. The example of the pool and the reflections was just to help you see how I can be totally distinct from the universe and yet at the same time intimately present in it. That's all. It wasn't meant to tell you anything else about me. So don't get hung up on the example. I'm *not* a pool and the universe is *not* a reflection.

LEN
Does that tie in with what you said earlier about human language being unable to cope with divine things?

GOD
It does indeed. I can only explain things to you if they make sense within your own experience. So I've got to use illustrations and examples that you understand. But an illustration is only an illustration and an example is only an example. They are not the real thing.

LEN
I see. In that case, can you give me an illustration that will help me to see what you meant when you said you hold the universe in existence at every moment? I find that hard to grasp.

GOD
Why?

LEN
Well, when human beings create something they make it and then they can walk away from it. A painter, for example, doesn't hold his painting in existence all the time, does he? He paints the picture, and then there it is, whether he's around or not.

GOD
I'll grant you that, Len. But it's not entirely true to say that *all* human creation is like that, is it?

LEN
What other way is there?

GOD
Well, think of a singer singing a song. The song lasts only as long as the singer is singing it. At every moment it depends entirely on the singer. If the singer stopped singing, the song would cease.

LEN
That's true. So are you saying that the universe is a sort of song you are singing?

GOD
You can put it like that if you want to. But remember, it's only an illustration. If it helps, that's fine. If it doesn't, forget it.

LEN
Actually, it seems to me to be a better illustration than the pool and the reflections.

GOD
In what way?

LEN
Well, a singer actively *creates* a song; and you create the universe.

GOD
Good point. Anything else you like about it?

LEN
I think it also preserves the idea that you are intimately present in the universe but also distinct from it.

GOD
How?

LEN
A singer is totally distinct from the song he sings. He can exist without the song, but the song can't exist without the singer. At the same time the singer and the song go together. There wouldn't be a song unless the singer was singing it.

GOD
Full marks, Len.

LEN
But there's still one thing puzzling me.

GOD
I was afraid there might be. What is it?

LEN
If you are intimately present to the universe, why is it we don't see any *evidence* of your presence?

GOD
What sort of evidence would you like?

LEN
I'm not sure really. But if you're as close as you say you are, surely there should be some way in which you make your presence felt?

GOD
Oh there is. But I've a feeling it's not quite what you're looking for. Can't you tell me what you have in mind?

LEN
Well, one or two divine manifestations would be a start.

GOD
Do you mean signs and wonders and things like that?

LEN
Along those lines, yes.

GOD
Do you really think it would help?

LEN
Yes, of course, it would give us an indication that you are there.

GOD
In what way?

LEN
By showing us there is something in the world that only you could have brought about.

GOD
And what sort of thing could that be?

LEN
Something spectacular, or unusual.

GOD
Like turning the sea orange, for example?

LEN
That sort of thing, yes.

GOD
But what would that prove?

LEN
It would prove that you were at work in the world.

GOD
But supposing scientists said, "The sea has turned orange and we don't know why at the moment, but eventually we will discover a natural cause for it."

LEN
They'd be wrong. It would be obvious that you had done it.

GOD
Why?

LEN
Because it would be too amazing to have a natural explanation.

GOD
Would it be more amazing than, say, punching a hole in the ozone layer?

LEN
Ah, but the hole in the ozone layer is due to natural causes. Or rather, it's due to our use of fossil fuels and aerosol sprays.

GOD
But if the sea turned orange wouldn't it be more logical to look for a similar explanation – either natural or man-made?

LEN
Er…Yes, I suppose so. But if we couldn't find one…

GOD
How long would you give yourselves to find one?

LEN
Hm. I see what you're getting at. As long as there's the possibility that something might have a natural explanation we can't jump to the conclusion that it's a sure sign of your direct intervention.

GOD
Correct.

LEN
But that makes it sound as though you are on the side of the scientists.

GOD
I am.

LEN
You are?

GOD
Of course. Why shouldn't I be?

LEN
I always thought science was the enemy of religion.

GOD
Whatever gave you that idea?

LEN
Well, science leaves you out.

GOD
I know. Quite right, too.

LEN
You don't mind if science leaves you out?

GOD
Of course not. It's not the job of science to look for me. Science studies the natural world, the universe as it is. It looks for explanations of what things are and how things happen and how things interact. It can do that perfectly well without any reference to me.

LEN
But if it leaves you out, doesn't it give a false picture?

GOD
Not in the least. No matter how hard you study the material universe you won't find me. I am not the answer to any scientific question. Science asks "What?" and "How?". I am the answer to a very different question.

LEN
And what question is that?

GOD
In view of all we've talked about up to now I think you ought to be able to answer that for yourself.

LEN
Yes, I suppose I should. But I must admit I'm all confused again.

GOD
Why?

LEN
First you say you are intimately present in the universe and then you say there's no way science can find you. It all seems a bit of a contradiction to me.

GOD
All right. Let's go back to our illustration of reflections in a pool. Imagine you're standing on the edge of the pool again. Now, if I asked you to make a list of everything you could see reflected in the pool, would you include the pool itself on the list?

LEN
No, of course not.

GOD
Why?

LEN
Because you asked for a list of *reflections* and the pool isn't a reflection.

GOD
Right. And if I asked you to make a list of all the things in the universe, would you include *me* on the list?

LEN
Er…I suppose the answer should be no.

GOD
It should indeed. But you don't seem very convinced.

LEN
It's just that I can't see why.

GOD
Think about it. If the pool is not a reflection, I am not…a what?

LEN
A created thing, I suppose.

GOD
Exactly. If you included me on a list of things in the universe you would be saying that I am a created thing.

LEN
Which you're not.

GOD
Which I most certainly am not.

LEN
Ah. I think I'm beginning to see what you're getting at. That must be why science can't find you. Science is only concerned with studying the material universe, with creation in other words; and you cannot be part of creation. Am I on the right lines?

GOD
You are, Len. And I hope it's clear to you why I cannot be the answer to any scientific question.

LEN
I think so. The questions science asks are questions about the created universe. But you are not part of the created universe, so science doesn't ask any questions about you.

GOD
Quite so.

LEN
But that brings me back to the point I made earlier. If you are not the answer to any scientific questions, what questions are you the answer to?

GOD
Let me give you a clue. What happens if a singer stops singing?

LEN
There is no song.

GOD
So if a song *is* being sung, what question does the singer answer?

LEN
Why is there a song?

GOD
Right. So, what question do I answer?

LEN
Why is there a universe?

GOD
You've got it. Or you could say I am the answer to the question: Why is there anything at all?

LEN
In other words, you are not the answer to questions about what happens in the universe. You are the answer to the question: Why is there something rather than nothing?

GOD
Exactly.

LEN
I can see that now. But there's still one thing niggling me.

GOD
What's that?

LEN
You are not part of the universe. You are not "in" the universe in the same sense as, say, planets are "in" the universe.

GOD
That's correct.

LEN
But nevertheless, you are intimately present to the universe.

GOD
Yes.

LEN
To use your own examples, you are as close to the universe as a pool to its reflections or a singer to his song. What I want to know is, why is your presence hidden from us?

GOD
Let me try to answer that with another illustration. Have you ever

hunted all over the house for your glasses only to discover eventually that you had them on all the time?

LEN
Funnily enough that happened to me yesterday. It was very frustrating.

GOD
Why was it so frustrating?

LEN
Because I spent ages looking for them when there was no necessity to look anywhere at all.

GOD
And why couldn't you see them?

LEN
I suppose it was because I was looking *through* them. They were too *close* to be seen.

GOD
Right. Now, that's why my presence is hidden from you. *I'm* too close to be seen.

LEN
I'm not sure I understand that.

GOD
All right, let me put it another way. How do you know you've got eyes?

LEN

Because I can see.

GOD

But have you ever seen your own eyes – directly, I mean? I'm not talking about seeing them in a mirror.

LEN

No, of course not. My eyes enable me to see, but obviously I can't see *them*.

GOD

Why is it so obvious?

LEN

Well, the things that enable you to see cannot possibly be seen by the one who sees.

GOD

Right. Now, just as your eyes enable you to see, so I enable you to exist. Just as your eyes are the condition for your seeing, so I am the condition for your being. And just as your own eyes must remain hidden from you, so must I remain hidden from you. As I said before, I am too close to you to be anything other than hidden.

LEN

If you're that close to us, why do we spend so much time searching for you?

GOD

I keep asking myself the same question.

FOR THOUGHT AND DISCUSSION

- How would you reply to someone who said, "Who made God?"
- Are science and religion opposed to each other?
- In what sense is it true to say, "God is totally distinct from us"?
- In what sense is it true to say, "God is intimately present to us"?
- God is like a singer and the universe is like his song. Is this a good illustration of creation? Has it any shortcomings?

Part Three

The void before creation; omnipotence and square circles; bringing back yesterday; God and sin.

LEN
There's one thing about you I've always wanted to know.

GOD
What's that?

LEN
What did you do before you created the universe?

GOD
What do you think I did?

LEN
I haven't a clue, really. But it must have been a very odd sort of existence.

GOD
Why? What do you think it was like?

LEN
Obviously I don't know. But I picture you floating around in a sort of black void for countless aeons, all on your own.

GOD
That certainly does sound odd.

LEN
Very boring, I should imagine.

GOD
I imagine it would be. And what do you think happened then?

LEN
Well, eventually you got tired of floating round in a black void on your own and decided to create the universe.

GOD
So that I wouldn't be so bored, you mean?

LEN
Something like that.

GOD
I'm glad this is all a figment of your imagination, Len.

LEN
You mean it wasn't like that?

GOD
Not quite.

LEN
What was it like, then?

GOD
Before I created the universe?

LEN
Yes.

GOD
The fact is, Len, there *wasn't* any time before I created the universe.

LEN
What do you mean?

GOD
I mean it doesn't make sense to ask what I did before I created the universe.

LEN
Why not?

GOD
For the simple reason that time is just as much part of creation as everything else in the universe. Time came into being with the universe. So it doesn't make sense to ask what I did before I created it. There wasn't any "before". Time did not exist.

LEN
But I always thought you were eternal.

GOD
And what do you think that means?

LEN
It means you had no beginning. You go back and back and back and back, to infinity. And you have no end either. You'll go on and on and on and on, without end.

GOD
Well, it's certainly true to say I have no beginning and no end, but that doesn't mean I go back and back and back, or on and on and on.

LEN
What does it mean, then?

GOD
It means that I exist outside time.

LEN
I'm not sure I understand what that means.

GOD
What it means is that although I act upon time, I am not myself measured by time.

LEN
So you don't go on and on and on?

GOD
No. I just *am*!

LEN
Why do we talk about everlasting life, then, if it isn't everlasting?

GOD
Because you have got to talk in terms you understand. You live in time and you don't know what it could possibly mean to live outside time. So you have to describe things as best you can. I did warn you at the very beginning of this conversation that I wouldn't be able to explain everything to you, didn't I?

LEN
True enough.

GOD
Well, this is one of the things it is impossible to explain.

LEN
I don't think I could ever understand it.

GOD
You will, in time…sorry, out of time.

LEN
It must be marvellous being almighty.

GOD
Do you really think so?

LEN
Oh, yes.

GOD
In what way?

LEN
Well, being able to do anything at all you want to.

GOD
Do you think I can do anything at all I want to?

LEN
Of course you can. You are God. You are almighty. You are all-powerful. It's obvious that you can do anything you want to.

GOD
All right, then. Do you think I could eat a plate of spaghetti bolognese if I felt like it?

LEN
Yes… er… No. I don't know. I've never really thought about it.

GOD
Think about it now.

LEN
I don't suppose you could.

GOD
You don't seem very sure.

LEN

I'm not. It just seems silly, you eating a plate of spaghetti bolognese, but I'm not sure why.

GOD

Well, let me give you a clue. If I ate enough plates of spaghetti bolognese, do you think I would put on weight?

LEN

No, of course not.

GOD

Why?

LEN

You haven't got a body; you can't put on weight.

GOD

Exactly. And that's why I can't eat spaghetti bolognese in the first place. In fact I can't do anything that involves physical activity or physical change. I can't go to Morecambe for my holidays, for example.

LEN

You wouldn't want to, though, would you?

GOD

That's true. But even if I wanted to I couldn't.

LEN

But doesn't that mean you're not all-powerful?

GOD

Not at all. It just means that I'm not part of the created, material universe. I am not bound by the limitations of physical beings.

LEN

I see. So, when I said you can do anything you want to I should really have qualified it a bit?

GOD

Correct. I am almighty in what I do. But nothing can be done to me; nothing can *change* me.

LEN

In that case, would it be true to say you are all-powerful because you can bring anything at all into existence?

GOD

It depends what you mean by "anything at all".

LEN

But if you are God, and if you are all-powerful, surely there is nothing you can't create?

GOD

And what do you think that means?

LEN

It means you can create anything at all…

GOD

You're going round in circles, Len. I've already said that it depends on what you mean by "anything at all".

LEN

All right, I've got an idea. I hope this doesn't sound impertinent, but can I challenge you to create something?

GOD
Create something? Here and now?

LEN
Yes.

GOD
You realise this is right outside normal procedures?

LEN
Oh yes. But, after all, this is *my* dream so I should have some say in what happens in it.

GOD
Fair enough. What would you like me to create?

LEN
A square circle.

GOD
A square circle. Are you sure?

LEN
Yes.

GOD
What will that prove?

LEN
It will prove you can create anything at all. It will prove you are all-powerful.

GOD
Will it really?

LEN
It will for me, anyway.

GOD
Let me get this straight, Len. You think that if I create a square circle it will prove I'm all-powerful?

LEN
I'd put it the other way round. If you *can't* create a square circle it will prove that you're *not* all-powerful.

GOD
So my omnipotence hinges on this?

LEN
You could put it like that, yes.

GOD
Phew! I'd better come up with the goods, then, hadn't I?

LEN
I think you better had.

GOD
Right. One square circle coming up. Oh, before I create it, just to make sure I'm going to get it right, could you describe a square circle for me?

LEN
Describe it?

GOD
Yes.

LEN
Er…No, I don't think I could.

GOD
Why not?

LEN
Because I can't imagine what a square circle would be like.

GOD
What's the difficulty in imagining it?

LEN
It's beyond my powers of imagination.

GOD
But you don't think it's beyond *my* powers of imagination?

LEN
No, of course, not. You're God. Nothing can be beyond your powers of imagination. You can know things and do things that are beyond human understanding.

GOD
Well, it's certainly true that I can know things and do things beyond human understanding, but does a square circle come into that category?

LEN
Yes.

GOD
Are you sure?

LEN
Yes, why, shouldn't it?

GOD
Let me ask you this. What is a circle?

LEN
It's a shape that's perfectly round.

GOD
So it's got no corners in it?

LEN
Right.

GOD
But a square has got corners, hasn't it?

LEN
Oh yes. Four.

GOD
So you are asking me to create a geometrical shape that has got no corners in it and yet at the same time has four corners in it?

LEN
Yes.

GOD
A shape with four corners and no corners at the same time?

LEN
Er… Yes.

GOD
What does that sound like to you?

LEN
I have to admit it sounds like a contradiction.

GOD
It *is* a contradiction. And a contradiction is not something that's very difficult to do, nor is it something beyond human understanding; a contradiction is a form of words which fails to describe anything which could exist.

LEN
So you *can't* create a square circle.

GOD
It's got nothing to do with my power to create, Len. It's
simply that a square circle is a logical contradiction. You couldn't describe a square circle to me because the expression "square circle" does not describe *anything*.

LEN
But I've always been taught that everything is possible for you.

GOD

Everything which is *possible* is possible for me. I can do things which human beings can't do. I can do things which it would be very difficult for human beings to do. But things which are not possible in themselves, because they involve a contradiction, simply cannot be done.

LEN

What about miracles, then?

GOD

What about them?

LEN

Don't *they* involve a contradiction?

GOD

Give me an example of a miracle that involves a contradiction.

LEN

Well, bringing a dead person back to life.

GOD

What is the contradiction in that?

LEN

It's not a common occurrence, is it?

GOD

I'll grant you that. But saying it doesn't happen very often is not the same as saying it involves a contradiction.

LEN

But *I* couldn't bring a dead person back to life, could I?

GOD

True enough. But that's because you haven't got the power to do so, not because a dead person coming back to life is a contradiction. It *would* be a contradiction if I said I could make a person to be alive and dead at the same time. But there's no contradiction in a person who was once dead being brought back to life.

LEN

So your power only extends to doing things which it is possible to do?

GOD

My power *can* only extend to things which it is possible to do. But that does not mean my power is in any way restricted. It simply means that if you ask me to do something which is logically impossible, the limitation lies in your words not in my power.

LEN

What if I asked you to bring back yesterday, could you do that?

GOD

Why should you want to bring back yesterday?

LEN

Supposing I wanted to change a decision I'd made?

GOD

In the light of what I've just been saying you should be able to answer your own question…

LEN

I'm not sure that I can.

GOD

All right. Tell me something you did yesterday.

LEN

Er…I went for a haircut.

GOD

Fine. Now let's suppose it was a terrible haircut and you want me to bring back yesterday so that you can change your mind about going to the barber.

LEN
Right.

GOD
Now. Is it true to say you had a haircut yesterday?

LEN
Yes, it is.

GOD
But if I brought back yesterday and you did not go to the barber it would be false to say you had a haircut yesterday. Am I right?

LEN
Yes.

GOD
But we've already established that you *did* have a haircut yesterday. So we would be forced into saying that it is both true and false that you had a haircut yesterday, which is absurd. Again we are faced with a contradiction.

LEN
So, you can't bring back yesterday?

GOD
Let's be precise, Len. Yesterday cannot be brought back. That which has in fact happened cannot be made *not* to have happened.

LEN
I see. But there's one more thing bothering me.

GOD
What's that?

LEN
We've been talking about you being all-powerful. What I want to know is: can you commit sin?

GOD
What do you think?

LEN
I've always been taught that you can't.

GOD
You've been taught correctly.

LEN
But if you can't commit sin it means there's something you can't do. Therefore you are not all-powerful.

GOD
Ah, an interesting point, Len. Let me start by asking you what sin is.

LEN
It's doing something wrong.

GOD
You mean like parking on a double yellow line?

LEN
No, not that kind of wrong.

GOD
What kind, then?

LEN
It's got to be a wrong that's against your will.

GOD
Right. Now, why do you think certain things are against my will?

LEN
Er…Is it because you want to test us?

GOD
What do you mean?

LEN
You want to see whether we will obey you, so you make it clear that some things are against your will.

GOD
You mean, if I say it is against my will that you lie or steal I'm saying that to test you, to see if you'll obey?

LEN
Yes.

GOD
What an odd idea.

LEN
Why is it odd?

GOD
Well, if my purpose is to test you, surely I could just as easily have said that it's against my will that you wear brown shoes, to see if you'd obey that?

LEN
Ah. I don't think that's true.

GOD
I should hope it isn't. Come on, Len. Think again. Why are certain things like lying and stealing against my will?

LEN
Is it because they harm other people?

GOD
That's a bit better. But there's more to it than that. What is happening when you steal something from someone?

LEN
I'm failing to respect their property.

GOD
Correct. Anything else?

LEN
I suppose I'm failing to respect the people I steal from, too.

GOD
Good. Anything else?

LEN
You could also say I'm failing to respect myself.

GOD
Why?

LEN
Because I'm being greedy and selfish; or because I want something without being prepared to pay for it or work for it.

GOD
Would you say that being greedy and selfish is a power that you have?

LEN
No, not at all. It's a deficiency in my character. A weakness.

GOD
Right. So, now can you see why I don't want you to sin?

LEN
Is it because you don't want me to have a deficiency in my character?

GOD
It's because I don't want you to have any deficiency at all. I want you to be a fully mature human being: as whole and as perfect and as

happy as you can be.

LEN
I've never realised that before.

GOD
It's true, Len. And now can you perhaps also begin to see why my inability to commit sin in no way calls into question my almighty power?

LEN
You mean, sin is not a power at all?

GOD
Exactly. It's a failure, a deficiency, a lack of something. When you sin you fall short of what you should be.

LEN
And you *can't* fall short of what you should be?

GOD
Correct. In fact, it is precisely because I *am* all-powerful that I cannot sin.

FOR THOUGHT AND DISCUSSION

- What does it mean to say "God is eternal"?
- How can we know that God exists outside time?
- "With God all things are possible." What can you say about this statement?
- Could God make a Time Machine?
- How would you reply to someone who said, "If God can't sin, he can't be all-powerful"?

Part Four

Evil and suffering in the world; what makes bad things bad? Is God responsible?

LEN
You've explained why you cannot sin, but some people would say you have a lot to answer for.

GOD
In what way?

LEN
Well, you have created a world in which there is terrible suffering.

GOD
What sort of suffering?

LEN
All sorts: natural disasters, diseases and disabilities, not to mention the suffering people deliberately inflict on each other.

GOD
And what do you think all that proves?

LEN
Some people would say it proves you are not as good as you are made out to be. Others would say it proves that you don't exist at all.

GOD
What about you? What do you think it proves?

LEN
I must admit I do sometimes wonder about your goodness when I see the evil and suffering in the world. And sometimes I do wonder whether you are there at all. It's very puzzling to say the least.

GOD
Why?

LEN
It's obvious. If you are all-powerful, as you say you are, surely you could have created a world in which there was no suffering?

GOD
And why do you think I didn't?

LEN
I don't know. As I say, I find it very puzzling.

GOD
But you still believe in me?

LEN
Yes, I do. But, to be honest, you don't always make it easy.

GOD
How do you answer people who say evil and suffering prove that I don't exist?

LEN
With difficulty.

GOD
But you do have some answers?

LEN
Yes, but I'm not always very happy with them.

GOD
What are they?

LEN
Well, sometimes I say that the evil and suffering in the world, are your punishment on us for the wrongs we do.

GOD
Ouch! I'm glad you said you're not always happy with your answers.

LEN
You mean that's not a good one?

GOD
Frankly, Len, it's terrible.

LEN
Why?

GOD
Do you really think, when a baby suffers some illness, that I am punishing the child for some crime he or she has committed?

LEN
Er…No. I suppose not.

GOD
Definitely not.

LEN
Oh.

GOD
What else do you say?

LEN
I point out that a lot of the evil in the world is due to human beings with free will. *That* kind of evil at least can't be put down to you.

GOD
Nice try, Len. But you can't get me off the hook with that argument.

LEN
Can't I? Why not?

GOD
If you recall an earlier part of your dream, you'll remember that we established that I hold everything in existence at every moment. I cause everything at every moment. That means that I also cause the free actions of human beings.

LEN
How can they be free if you cause them?

GOD
What I mean is, that in acting freely you do not act independently of me. You can't; your very existence depends on me at every moment. So your free acts are also dependent on me.

LEN
So you have to take the rap for the evil people do?

GOD
Let me put it this way: you can't excuse me by putting the blame on people.

LEN
Now you've really got me puzzled. I knew the problem of evil and suffering in the world was a difficult one, but you've taken away the arguments I thought went at least some way towards explaining it.

GOD
If we're going to discuss this subject, Len, I want you to be clear about what you can and can't say about me.

LEN
So can we discuss it?

GOD
Certainly. Where do you want to start?

LEN
I just want an explanation.

GOD
All right, let's see what we can do. First of all, you said you find the presence of evil and suffering in the world very puzzling.

LEN
Yes. I can't square it with the idea that you are all-powerful and all-loving.

GOD
If it's any consolation to you, Len, there is a very important sense in which you are *right* to be puzzled. From one point of view there is no answer I can give you. There is a mystery of evil which is beyond comprehension. You would have to enter into the mystery of my very being to begin to understand it, and that is simply not open to you in your earthly life – not even in this dream of yours.

LEN
So you've got nothing to tell me about all the suffering in the world?

GOD

I didn't say that. I said there is a level at which you cannot comprehend the mystery of evil, but that does not mean there is nothing to be said about it.

LEN

What can you say about it, then?

GOD

I can say why it doesn't prove I am not good and loving. And I think I can show you that I do not directly bring about anything evil. I can also show you that I bring about everything that is good in the world. In other words, I can clear some of the ground for you. I can help you to understand where the problem of evil and suffering really lies and where it doesn't.

LEN

That would certainly be a help. Where do we begin?

GOD

Let's take it slowly. We'll start by thinking about what you mean when you say something is bad or evil. Let's stick to the word "bad" for the moment. Do you think there is such a thing as "badness"?

LEN

Just on its own?

GOD

Yes.

LEN

I've never really thought about it. But I don't suppose there is really. There are only bad things.

GOD

Right. Just as there is no such thing as tallness or blueness, but only tall things and blue things. Now, when you say something is bad what do you mean?

LEN

Er…I don't know, really.

GOD

Give me an example of something that you think is bad.

LEN
Our kettle is pretty bad.

GOD
What's bad about it?

LEN
It scalds your hand with steam when you pour boiling water from it.

GOD
Why does that make it a bad kettle?

LEN
Well, you don't expect a kettle to scald you, do you?

GOD
Right. So it's a bad kettle because it doesn't live up to your expectations of a kettle?

LEN
Yes.

GOD
Give me an example of something else that's bad.

LEN
The dentist told me yesterday I've got a bad tooth.

GOD
Is your tooth bad because it scalds you when you pour boiling water from it?

LEN
No, of course not. It's bad because it's decaying in the middle and I can't chew with it.

GOD
So the badness of your tooth is different from the badness of your kettle?

LEN
Yes.

GOD
What is the difference?

LEN
Well, the kettle's bad because it doesn't function properly as a kettle; and the tooth is bad because it doesn't function properly as a tooth.

GOD
Right. So when you say something is bad you've got to know what it *is* first. And its badness consists in not living up to your expectations of what it is.

LEN
Yes. But where's this all leading us?

GOD
Be patient, Len. I told you we've got to take it slowly. We're thinking about what we mean when we say something is bad. We've established that there is no such thing as badness in itself. There are only bad things. What else have we established?

LEN
We saw that we call something bad when it doesn't live up to our expectations of what it should be.

GOD
Can you explain that a bit further?

LEN

Well, take a goalkeeper, for example. You expect a goalkeeper to be able to catch a ball. If he couldn't, you'd say he was a bad goalkeeper. And you expect a boiled egg to taste like a boiled egg. If it tasted of marzipan you'd say it was a bad egg.

GOD

Right. So, when something is bad it fails to live up to your expectations of it. It is deficient in some way. Do you agree?

LEN

Yes, that's fairly clear.

GOD

So, to say something is bad is to say something negative about it.

LEN

Negative? Do you mean it has something missing?

GOD

No, I don't mean that. A thing can be deficient by having too much as well as too little.

LEN

How?

GOD

Well, think of an egg. It could be bad because it had gone off. But it could also be bad because someone had stubbed out their cigarette in it.

LEN

I see what you mean. So, a goalkeeper could be bad because he was too tall to get down quickly enough to the low shots?

GOD

Exactly. When you say something is bad you mean it lacks some positive quality. And that quality is something you expect the thing to have. You expect a goalkeeper to have the ability to get down to the low shots – at least some of the time; and you expect the edible part of an egg to consist of white and yolk only. If it doesn't, you say it's a bad egg.

LEN
But if you say badness is negative, doesn't that mean it is unreal?

GOD
No, not at all. The lack of what is to be expected of something is just as real as a presence.

LEN
I'm not sure I understand that.

GOD
Well, think of a tennis court. Supposing someone dug a big hole in the middle of it. If you tried to play tennis on it, it certainly wouldn't live up to your expectations of a tennis court, but the hole would be very real, it would not be an illusion.

LEN
I see.

GOD
One more point. For a thing to be bad it has to have at least some good in it. A bad egg has at least to be recognisable as an egg. A bad kettle has to succeed at least in being a kettle, otherwise you couldn't describe it as a bad kettle. Do you see what that means?

LEN
I can't say I do.

GOD
It means that you can't talk about a thing being totally bad. There always has to be some goodness in a thing. A thing that had nothing good about it at all simply would not exist.

LEN
I've never thought of that before.

GOD
That's one reason why I've been taking you through this exploration of what you mean when you say something is bad. Now we can move on to see what all this tells us about evil and suffering in the world. But before we do that, would you care to summarise where we've got to, Len?

LEN
If I've understood you correctly, there seem to be three points we can make about badness.

GOD
What are they?

LEN
First of all, badness is relative. A bad bicycle, for example, will not be bad for the same reason that a bad sausage roll is bad.

GOD
Right. And the second point?

LEN
The second point is that badness is negative. It is a lack or a deficiency in something. We say a thing is bad when it does not come up to our expectations of it, when it fails to be what we expect it to be.

GOD
Fine.

LEN
And the third point is that badness cannot exist without some goodness.

GOD
What does that mean?

LEN
It means that a thing has at least to be itself before we can say it is bad. So, to that extent at least, it is good.

GOD
Can you give me an example?

LEN
Well, a bad cheese-grater has at least to be a cheese-grater. You can't have the badness without the cheese-grater, in other words.

GOD
So you can't have badness without some goodness?

LEN
Yes.

GOD
But, if you think about it, you will realise that you can have goodness without any badness.

LEN
Yes, I suppose that's true.

GOD
Good. Now we can take the discussion a step further. Let's look at the evil or the badness in the world. The badness that affects things. I want to insist that I do not directly cause the bad or the evil that happens in the world. I do not directly will evil for its own sake. In the light of what we've said about badness can you see why?

LEN
I'm not sure that I can.

GOD
Think about the three points you've just made about badness and put them next to me as the creator, the cause of all things. Do you see anything odd about the idea of me causing evil?

LEN

Well, we've said that badness is negative, haven't we? It's a lack, a deficiency in something. A failure in a thing to be what we expect it to be.

GOD

You're on the right lines, Len. Do you think a lack or a deficiency can be created?

LEN

Er, no, I don't suppose it can. A deficiency is not a real thing, is it? As you've already said, badness in a thing means it is failing to be what we expect it to be. And failure cannot exist as an independent reality. So I suppose badness can't be created.

GOD

What does that say about the things I do create?

LEN

That they can't be bad.

GOD

Correct. I can't create badness because there is nothing to create. I can't *cause* badness because there is nothing to cause. Badness cannot exist on its own.

LEN

So everything you cause, everything you create, is good?

GOD

Yes. I can only cause what is good.

LEN

But you have created a world in which bad things can happen.

GOD

I'll grant you that, Len. But all I'm trying to do at the moment is to show you that I do not directly cause or create the badness or the evil in the world. But there's still a lot more to say on this subject.

LEN

That's good. Because I've still got more questions.

FOR THOUGHT AND DISCUSSION

- Can badness exist on its own?
- What does it mean to say something is bad?
- Think of some examples of bad things and say what is bad about them.
- God can't create anything bad. True or false?
- Is all the evil in the world due to human beings?
- How would you reply to someone who said, "The evil in the world is God's punishment on us"?

Part Five

The evil people suffer; the evil people do; free will and evil; has God failed us?

LEN
You said that everything you create is good and you can't create anything bad.

GOD
That's correct.

LEN
But if you are responsible for everything that exists, how is it that bad things happen in the world? I mean, there is suffering, there is evil. You can't deny that, can you?

GOD
No, I can't.

LEN
So how do you explain it?

GOD
We're going to have to take it slowly again, Len.

LEN
I thought we might have to.

GOD
First, let's think about the kinds of badness or evil that there are in the world. Give me an example, from your own experience, of something bad.

LEN
Er, let's see. I know. Last winter I got a terrible dose of flu. I was in bed for about ten days.

GOD
Right. That was a bad thing that happened to you.

LEN
Yes.

GOD
You had no say in the matter.

LEN
None at all. One day I was walking about quite happily, the next day I was knocked flat by a flu germ.

GOD
Now, Len, I don't want to embarrass you too much, but I'd like to remind you of another bad episode in your life in recent months.

LEN
What was that?

GOD
I'm thinking of the occasion when you backed your car into another one in a car park.

LEN
Oh, dear. I was hoping you hadn't noticed that.

GOD
I can understand why. You made a big dent in it, didn't you?

LEN
Be fair, it was an accident.

GOD

But it wasn't an accident that you drove off quickly without leaving your name and address under the windscreen-wiper, was it?

LEN

Er, no, it wasn't.

GOD

The owner had to pay for the damage himself instead of you, right?

LEN

Right.

GOD

Do you think that was a good thing to do, Len?

LEN

No. I'm very ashamed of it now.

GOD

Why?

LEN

Because it was unjust, I suppose.

GOD

Correct. Now I think we've got two examples of the different kinds of badness or evil that you find in the world. There are the bad things that happen to people (and to other creatures) – like your dose of flu. And there are the bad things that people do – like your episode in the car park. Agreed?

LEN

Are you sure that covers everything?

GOD

I think so. Can you think of any other kinds of badness or evil?

LEN

I can't say I can.

GOD

Right. Now, your question is this: If I, who am God, can only create what is good, why is there any badness or evil or suffering in the world at all?

LEN
Yes.

GOD
I think the best plan will be to try to answer that in two parts. First we'll look at the bad things that happen to people and to other creatures: the evil they *suffer*. Then later on we'll think about the bad things people *do*, moral evil or sin. All right?

LEN
Fine. But surely a lot of the evil in the world is brought about by the malice of people? So the evil *suffered* and the evil people *do* is often the same thing.

GOD
Some of it is; but I wouldn't say a lot of it is. If you think about it, only a small proportion of the evil in the world can be put down to the malice of people.

LEN
How do you mean?

GOD
Well, for one thing, the human race has only been in existence for a very short period of the world's history. Before mankind ever appeared on the scene animals preyed on each other and natural disasters occurred. None of that could be put down to the malice of human beings. It is the same today. Diseases and disabilities, for example, can't be put down to the malice of human beings.

LEN
I see what you mean. But that means we've got to put the evil down to you, doesn't it?

GOD
No. I've already told you I can't create anything evil.

LEN
Well how does it get there, then?

GOD
Think about it like this. What did you have for your Sunday dinner?

LEN
Roast chicken.

GOD
Did you enjoy it?

LEN
Yes, it was wonderful. My wife, Pat, is a very good cook.

GOD
Do you think it was *good* for you? The chicken, I mean.

LEN
Yes, of course.

GOD
In what way?

LEN
Well, we need food to live and develop, don't we? And it tasted good, too.

GOD
Now, do you think it was good for the chicken?

LEN
What?

GOD
You eating it for your Sunday dinner.

LEN
I never really thought about it.

GOD
Well, think about it now. Was it good for the chicken?

LEN
No, of course not.

GOD
It was definitely *bad* for the chicken. In that case, do you think you were doing anything evil when you ate it?

LEN
No. Eating chicken is natural, isn't it?

GOD
So, you did no evil when you ate the chicken for Sunday dinner, but the result was still very bad for the chicken, right?

LEN
Right.

GOD
Do you see what that means?

LEN
I suppose it means that the evil done to the chicken can't be helped. Unless, of course, we all became vegetarians.

GOD
Nice try, Len. But that won't solve the problem. If you don't harm chickens you'll have to harm something else: carrots, for example. The fact is, you cannot be what you are, you cannot perfect yourself, without destroying some other part of the world. And that holds true throughout nature.

LEN
So, what's bad news for one thing may be good news for something else?

GOD
You've got it.

LEN
But the harm I do does not mean I myself am wicked or evil.

GOD
Of course not.

LEN
So, I harm certain things, not because I am evil, but because I have to harm them in order to live and develop as a human being?

GOD
Yes. And, of course, the same is true the other way round.

LEN
How do you mean?

GOD
When other creatures harm *you* it is not because *they* are evil in themselves but because they are growing and developing in *their* way.

LEN
Wait a minute. If someone hits me on the head with a hammer I'd say there's a very good chance that they are evil in themselves.

GOD
I agree. But remember, we're not at the moment talking about *that* kind of evil – the evil people *do*. We'll come to that later. We're talking about the kind of evil that *happens* to people.

LEN
Ah.

GOD
For example, think of that dose of flu you had last winter. How did you feel while it lasted?

LEN
Terrible.

GOD
Now, I know this is no consolation at all, Len, and I'm reluctant to mention it, but all the while you were feeling terrible the flu germ was having a wonderful time.

LEN
Eh?

GOD
Sorry about that, but it's true. In harming you the germ was developing and growing, just as in harming a chicken by eating it you are developing and growing.

LEN
I see. So, when I had flu and felt terrible, something bad was happening to me; but the badness didn't come from the germ being evil in itself. The germ was simply doing its own thing: being a good little germ, in other words?

GOD
You've got it.

LEN
But you created the germ.

GOD
True. But not as an evil thing. I created it to be a good little germ.

LEN
But why create germs at all?

GOD
Chickens that get eaten for Sunday dinner might just as easily ask the question: Why create human beings?

LEN

I've never thought of that. But you seem to be saying that evil in the world is inevitable.

GOD

It is unavoidable in a material world in which life evolves and grows.

LEN

And you allow it to happen.

GOD

In causing the good in the world I have to allow for the fact that some evil will occur. But I don't *cause* the evil.

LEN

Then why make a world like that in the first place?

GOD

Would you rather I *hadn't* created the world?

LEN

No, but why couldn't you have created it in a way that did not entail creatures damaging each other in order to live?

GOD

How could I have done that?

LEN

Well, for one thing you could miraculously feed every creature so that they didn't need to damage other creatures for food.

GOD

But in that case you would have a world without any natural order. Things would not happen because of natural causes but because of my miracles. In such a world scientific investigation would be impossible because you'd never know what was a miracle and what was natural. Would you want that kind of world?

LEN

I suppose not.

GOD

Len, I am not pretending that what I've said is any consolation to people who suffer evil. I don't console by arguments. I have other ways. I'm just trying to show you that the evil in the world does not prove I am not good, or that I do not exist.

LEN
Yes, I can see that now. But that's only one kind of evil, isn't it? – the evil that happens to people. We've still got to talk about the other kind of evil, haven't we? – the evil people do of their own free will.

GOD
Which is another way of saying moral evil, or sin. Right?

LEN
Right.

GOD
What do you think we can say about this kind of evil, Len?

LEN
I think I can understand this kind of evil more easily.

GOD
Do you, indeed? Why?

LEN
Well, the evil that people do is done of their own free will. So it is obviously down to *them*, not down to *you*.

GOD
Do you think I want them to do evil?

LEN
No, of course not.

GOD
Then why don't I stop them?

LEN
Because it would be taking away their freedom. Even though we sometimes commit horrible crimes it is better that we should be free to do so than that we should be programmed automatons.

GOD
Sorry, Len, but that line of argument simply won't do.

LEN
Won't it? Why not?

GOD
Remember what we said earlier in our conversation when we were talking about creation. You depend on me for your existence at every moment. You cannot exist apart from me; you cannot act apart from me. I am the cause of your free actions just as I am the cause of everything else in creation.

LEN
How can I be free if I'm dependent on you?

GOD
Freedom does not mean that you are independent of me. You can never be that. Freedom means you are independent of other people and other created things.

LEN
So if I do something wrong, you have caused it?

GOD
In a sense, yes. You could not have done the action without me. But I am not the cause of your wrongdoing. I do not cause you to sin. The action still springs from your freedom of will.

LEN
But aren't we back to what I said earlier? You allow me to sin to preserve my freedom.

GOD
No.

LEN
Why not?

GOD
For the simple reason that I could prevent you from sinning without destroying your freedom.

LEN
You could?

GOD
Oh, yes.

LEN
Then why don't you?

GOD
We'll come back to that later. At the moment I just want you to be clear that you can't defend moral evil by saying it has at least one good aspect to it: namely, that it is an inevitable consequence of human freedom. Moral evil is not a consequence of human freedom. Moral evil, or sin, has nothing good about it at all.

LEN
Then how can you possibly defend it? When we were talking about the evil in the world we were at least able to see that the evil that happens to one creature is contributing to the good of another. But if moral evil has no good in it, no one is benefiting at all.

GOD
That's absolutely right, Len.

LEN
But why is there no benefit?

GOD
The reason is that moral evil, sin, is self-inflicted evil.

LEN
Self-inflicted?

GOD
Yes. When you sin you harm yourself.

LEN
But I always thought things were wrong because they harmed other people.

GOD
Not so, Len. An action of yours may be wrong because it harms others, but what makes it morally wrong is the harm it does to yourself.

LEN
I'm not sure I understand that.

GOD
All right. Let's take an example. We'll go back to your adventure in the car park.

LEN
Oh, no. Not again, please.

GOD
Don't worry about it. You are forgiven for what you did. But it makes a convenient example.

LEN
Very well.

GOD
What happened was that you bashed another car, saw what you'd done, and drove off without leaving your name and address. So the driver of the damaged car had to pay for the repairs.

LEN
Yes.

GOD
Now why was your action morally wrong?

LEN
Because I was acting unjustly.

GOD
Right. Now supposing, when you bashed the other car, you *hadn't* noticed. Let's say you drove away completely oblivious to the damage you'd done. Would *that* have been morally wrong?

LEN
No, of course not.

GOD
And yet the harm to the other driver would have been exactly the same. He would still have had to fork out and pay for the damage.

LEN
I see what you're getting at. The moral wrong consisted in me acting unjustly, not in the fact that the other driver was harmed.

GOD
Exactly. Your unjust action was a defect in *you*. It diminished *you*. In that moment you made yourself less of a human being. In other words, you inflicted evil on yourself.

LEN
And all moral evil, all sin, is like that?

GOD
It is. And the thing to notice is that because it is self-inflicted there can be no good in it at all.

LEN
Why not?

GOD
You remember when you had the flu. It was very bad for you, but very good for the flu germ. But when you sin the evil you do is self-inflicted; there is no other being which benefits. It's a dead loss all round. Mind you, I can bring good out of the evil you do, but your evil actions *in themselves* have no good in them at all.

LEN
But that puts *you* in a bit of a spot, doesn't it?

GOD
Why?

LEN
Well, when we were talking about the evil people suffer you said it was an unavoidable part of the material universe, because in growing and developing living things inevitably harm each other. What's bad for one thing is good for something else.

GOD
So?

LEN
You can't say that about moral evil, can you? You've just said yourself that there's no good in it at all.

GOD
True enough.

LEN
Well, you can't deny there *is* moral evil in the world, so don't we have to say you are responsible for it?

GOD
Sorry to return to this, Len, but in what way did we agree your action in the car park was harmful to you?

LEN
It was a defect in me. I was failing to live up to what a human being should be.

GOD
So it was an absence of something?

LEN
Yes.

GOD
Well, how could I create an absence? How could I create a defect, a failure?

LEN
I see what you mean. The failure was all down to me.

GOD
I'm afraid so, Len.

LEN
But you said earlier that you could have prevented me from failing.

GOD
Yes, I could.

 LEN
Then why didn't you?

GOD
Why do you think I didn't?

LEN
Is it because you didn't want to take away my freedom?

GOD
Len, how many more times have I got to tell you? Your freedom means you can act independently of other creatures. It does not mean that you can act independently of me. I am the source of your free actions just as I am the source of your very existence. You are free because of me, not in spite of me.

LEN
So you don't have to let me sin in order to leave me with my freedom?

GOD
No. I could have created a world in which everyone was free but no-one sinned.

LEN
Then why didn't you?

GOD
Why should I have?

LEN
Well I'd be happier and everyone else would be happier if there was no sin in the world.

GOD
That's true.

LEN
Then surely you've got an obligation to make a world in which there is no sin?

GOD
To whom have I got an obligation?

LEN
To us, of course.

GOD
Do you think I had an obligation to create you in the first place?

LEN
No, I suppose not.

GOD
Then why do you think I've got an obligation to prevent you from sinning?

LEN
All right, I take your point. You are God, and you can't have an obligation to anyone. But the question still remains. If you can prevent us from sinning without interfering with our freedom, why don't you?

GOD
You may remember that when we started talking about the evil

and suffering that exist in the world I said that there is a mystery here which is beyond your comprehension.

LEN
Yes, I remember.

GOD
We have now reached that point, Len.

LEN
You mean you won't tell me why you permit us to sin?

GOD
It's not that I *won't*, Len; it's that you wouldn't understand it if I did.

LEN
But surely you can put it into simple words?

GOD
I can; but you wouldn't understand the simple words.

LEN
Why not?

GOD
Think back to an example we used right at the beginning of our conversation. I asked you whether, using doggy language, you could explain to your dog what you were doing when you were reading the newspaper. Remember?

LEN
Yes.

GOD
And what was your answer?

LEN
I said I couldn't.

GOD
Why?

LEN
Because a dog's experience is limited to doggy things. A dog simply could not cope with human concepts and ideas.

GOD

Exactly. In the same way, only much more so, human intellects can't cope with divine things. At some point you have to accept, Len, that I am a mystery to you. A complete mystery. You cannot know anything about my nature or my purposes. Not because I won't tell you, but because they are beyond your comprehension.

LEN

So the problem of evil has to remain a mystery to me?

GOD

The reason why there is *sin* has to remain a mystery to you. But I hope you understand a bit better why there is suffering in the world. And I hope you can see that I do not directly bring about any of the suffering or evil in the world. You can't understand why I permit sin. That will always be beyond your comprehension in your earthly life; it will always remain a mystery. I know that's not very satisfactory for you, but it would be very surprising if you could fathom the depths of my infinite will, wouldn't it? In the meantime, just remember this: whatever happens, I love you and I desire your complete happiness.

FOR THOUGHT AND DISCUSSION

■ In a material world which evolves and develops in time, some evil is inevitable. True or false?

■ God is not responsible for what people do of their own free will. True or false?

■ How would you respond to someone who said, "It is better to have free will and to sin than to be a programmed automaton"?

■ Sin is self-inflicted evil. Do you agree with this statement?

■ Moral evil has no good in it at all. Discuss this statement.

■ How would you reply to someone who said, "The evil in the world proves there is no God"?

■ God is the creator of everything, but there is evil in the world, therefore God must be the creator of evil. True or false?

Part Six

The meaning of mystery; God and creatures; the human and the divine; Father, Son and Holy Spirit.

LEN

You said I can never know you as you are in yourself, and I can never know your purposes.

GOD

Correct.

LEN

But what about this conversation? I thought you *had* been telling me about yourself.

GOD

Not really, Len. I haven't said anything that you couldn't have worked out on your own. In a way, you *have* worked it out on your own.

LEN

How do you mean?

GOD

Well, this is *your* dream, Len, not mine.

LEN

I see.

GOD

In this dream I've simply been guiding you through some of the things you can know about me by the use of human reason. But I haven't increased your knowledge of me as I am in myself. You *can't* know me like that. I am, and must always remain, a mystery to you.

LEN

But why? Why can't you let me in on the mystery? Why can't you explain it?

GOD

Because mysteries can't be explained. That's why they're mysteries.

LEN

But surely you can give me some indication, some clue.

GOD

All right, Len, I'll make a deal with you. I'll let *you* in on the mystery of *my* being if you'll let *me* in on the being of your wife, Pat.

LEN

How do you mean?

GOD

Well, if you tell me all about *her*, I'll tell you all about *me*. Fair enough?

LEN

Yes, fair enough.

GOD

Right, off you go then. Tell me all about Pat.

LEN

Well, let's see… she's about five foot two. She's got darkish hair; blue eyes. She'll be thirty-nine in September; she's average build. Er…

GOD

Anything else?

LEN

She's good at knitting; she likes a game of badminton occasionally; she's got a flair with potted plants; she likes reading Ruth Rendell thrillers…

GOD

Fine. Anything else?

LEN

She likes a good rummage round Marks and Spencer's on Saturday morning…

GOD

You're telling me *all* about her, remember?

LEN
Oh, yes. Well… she's very easy-going. She hardly ever gets angry about anything. She's very thoughtful; she likes doing things to please or surprise people. She's got a lot of patience.

GOD
Anything on the minus side?

LEN
She's a bit shy and lacking in confidence. She lets people walk over her sometimes; she won't stick up for herself. Oh, and she's useless at reading maps.

GOD
Anything else?

LEN
Er…She's very loyal… very good with children… er…

GOD
Anything else?

LEN
Er… Well, I'm sure there's lots more I could say, but I can't think of it at the moment.

GOD
Right…Now the deal was that if you told me all about Pat, I'd tell you all about me, right?

LEN
Right.

GOD
So, do you think you've told me all about Pat?

LEN
Er… No, not really. As I said, I'm sure there's a lot more I could say.

GOD
Supposing I gave you a couple more hours to think about it, do you think at the end of that time you would be able to tell me all about Pat?

LEN
To be honest, no. I don't suppose I would.

GOD
Why, what would be missing?

LEN
I'm not sure. There's just more to her than what I've said.

GOD
And more to her than *anything* you could say?

LEN
Yes.

GOD
And what is that "more"?

LEN
I don't know really. I can't explain it. It's just *her*. Herself.

GOD
A mystery in other words.

LEN
Pardon?

GOD
A mystery, Len. It's not only *I* who am a mystery to you. Mysteries surround you everywhere you look. At the heart of their being every other person is a mystery to you. You are even a mystery to

yourself. Do you see now why I can't explain the mystery of *my* being to you?

LEN

You mean, if I can't explain Pat, if her being is beyond explanation, then how much more must *you* be beyond explanation?

GOD

Quite so. The things I've been telling you about myself during this conversation are a bit like your descriptions of Pat. They're true as far as they go, but they miss out the central thing. They *have* to miss it out, for at the centre there is mystery. I am beyond words, I am beyond explanation, I must always remain an unfathomable mystery to you.

LEN

So, I *can't* know you as you are in yourself?

GOD

Correct.

LEN

But I *do* know Pat, even though I can't fully explain her in words.

GOD

Good point, Len. Let's pursue it. Do you know her *completely*?

LEN

No, not *completely*. But my knowledge of her is deeper than I can put into words. I mean, I love her. My love isn't for the *qualities* I've described. My love is for the *person*, for *Pat* herself.

GOD

She still remains a mystery to you, but because you have a loving relationship with her, you do enter to some extent into the mystery of her being.

LEN

Yes.

GOD

Now, Len, in a similar way – although you cannot know me as I am in myself – you *can* enter into a loving relationship with *me*.

LEN
Can I? I don't see how.

GOD
Why not?

LEN
Well, during this conversation you've talked about yourself as the *creator*, as the *cause* of everything that exists, as the *source* of all my actions, and so on. I don't see how I can have a loving relationship with a "creator" or a "cause" or a "source".

GOD
Good point, Len. You can have a loving relationship with Pat because you and she are equals. But if I am the creator and you are a creature there is an infinite gulf between us. We exist on a different plane. There's a much greater gulf between you and me than there is, say, between you and your dog. And you wouldn't say you had a loving relationship with your dog, would you?

LEN
No. Though I am *fond* of my dog; and I *care* for it.

GOD
Yes, but you wouldn't say you *love* your dog.

LEN
Some people *do* say they love their dogs.

GOD
Yes, but they're not using the word "love" in its true sense, are they? They wouldn't say they were *in love* with their dog, would they?

LEN
True. But that brings me back to my question: How can I have a loving relationship with you if the gulf between us is much greater than that between me and my dog?

GOD
What would have to happen to your dog to enable it to have a relationship with you?

LEN

It would have to become human, I suppose. Like a frog changing into a prince.

GOD

Right. So, what would have to happen to *you* to enable you to have a loving relationship with *me*?

LEN

I would have to become divine?

GOD

Exactly.

LEN

But that's impossible.

GOD

Impossible, Len? Where's your faith?

LEN

My faith?

GOD

Yes, your faith. Up to now in this conversation we've been talking chiefly about things you can know about me by human reason. At this point we must move into the realm of faith. You do have faith, Len, don't you?

LEN

Er…Yes. I think so. I hope so.

GOD

And what does your faith tell you about me?

LEN

That you are a God of love.

GOD

And that I love you?

LEN

Yes.

GOD

Good. Now what must that mean, in the light of what we've just been saying?

LEN

It must mean that, in some way, I am divine.

GOD

Exactly.

LEN

But that's astounding.

GOD

It is, Len, but it shouldn't be completely new to you: not if you have faith.

LEN

Why not?

GOD

Because the truth that you share in my divine life is at the very *heart* of your faith.

LEN

Yes, I suppose it is. But, I must say, I've never thought of it in quite that way before. And it raises another question: How do I become divine?

GOD

It's catechism time, Len. You should know the answer to that one.

LEN
Is it to do with Jesus, your Son, becoming man?

GOD
It is indeed. What can you tell me about Jesus?

LEN
He was both human and divine.

GOD
Correct. And do you think I love Jesus; do you think I loved him during his life on earth?

LEN
Yes, of course.

GOD
Do you see what that means? In Jesus I find a human being I can love because he is my equal. He is already divine.

LEN
Like the gospel says: "This is my beloved Son"?

GOD
Quite so. In Jesus the divine and the human meet.

LEN
You mean if Jesus, who is divine, was united to humanity, then humanity can be united to God: to you?

GOD
Through Jesus, humanity is united to me.

LEN
But how do we know that?

GOD
By faith. By faith you accept Jesus' offer of love and friendship, and because he is my beloved Son you are drawn into the life of love that exists between us. And that love is the Holy Spirit, who is also divine, poured into your heart.

LEN
But Jesus shares your divine life from all eternity, doesn't he?

GOD
Yes.

LEN
But we aren't divine in that sense.

GOD
No. The divine life you share in is given as a *gift*. That is what you mean by grace: my divine life given to you.

LEN
It all sounds a bit complicated.

GOD
It's a mystery, Len. You are drawn into my life of love, but in the darkness of faith not in the light of understanding.

LEN
You mean, after all you've said, I'm still none the wiser?

GOD
You're none the wiser about *me*. I can't remind you often enough that I must always remain a mystery to you. But I hope you're a bit wiser about *yourself*.

LEN
I think so. At any rate, I think I understand a bit more how I relate to you.

GOD
Good.

LEN
And the mystery you spoke of is the mystery of the Blessed Trinity?

GOD
It is.

LEN
You know, I'd always thought of the doctrine of the Trinity as a kind of puzzle to test our faith.

GOD
And now?

LEN
From what you've been saying, there seems to be a bit more to it than that.

GOD
I'm glad you think so, Len. What have you learned?

LEN
For one thing, it makes it possible for us to say that you are a God of love.

GOD
Why?

LEN
Because it means that within your divine life there is relation. You are not monolithic and alone.

GOD
But I *am* one God?

LEN
Oh yes. But your divine life is a life of love: Father, Son and Holy Spirit, loving each other from all eternity.

GOD
Which is another way of saying I *am* love. And I invite you to share in my love.

LEN
Yes. That's the wonderful part about it. It puts a new perspective on the doctrine of the Blessed Trinity for me.

GOD
In what way?

LEN
It helps me to see that you have created *me* for love. My destiny is one of love.

GOD
It is, Len. And it has already begun. For my love fills you now, and my love for you is everlasting.

FOR THOUGHT AND DISCUSSION

■ What is the difference between a puzzle and a mystery?

■ How much can we know about the nature of God?

■ Can the creator love his creatures?

■ How do we know that God is love?

■ Is the doctrine of the Incarnation essential to Christianity?

■ Is the doctrine of the Blessed Trinity essential to Christianity?

■ Human beings are made for love. True or false?

Part Seven

Is anybody listening? Can prayers be answered? Is it all right to ask for things? The heart of prayer.

LEN
I'd like to ask you about prayer.

GOD
What do you want to know?

LEN
I'd like to know if there's any point in praying.

GOD
Why shouldn't there be?

LEN
Well, to put it bluntly – and I hope you won't mind my saying this – it seems very hard to get through to you in prayer.

GOD
What makes you say that?

LEN
I should have thought it was fairly obvious. Most prayers don't seem to get answered.

GOD
And why do you think that is?

LEN
To be perfectly honest, it sometimes seems to me that you're not listening. We can pray and pray for something and nothing at all happens. You seem so distant and, as I said before, so hard to get through to.

GOD
And if you *did* get through, what would you want me to do?

LEN
To step in and answer my prayers, of course.

GOD
You mean like waving a magic wand to make everything all right?

LEN
That sort of thing, yes.

GOD
Oh, Len, you seem to have forgotten everything we've talked about up to now. You're going right back to your idea of me as someone standing outside the universe watching over it and waiting to step in if something goes wrong.

LEN
Yes, I am, aren't I? I was forgetting. You're *not* like that, are you?

GOD
No, I'm not. Can you remember why?

LEN
You said you can't step in because you are already in.

GOD
Exactly. I am always intimately present in the universe. I am the source of everything that exists at every moment.

LEN
But doesn't that mean that everything in creation is the way it is in accordance with your will?

GOD
Yes, it does.

LEN
In that case there's certainly no point in praying.

GOD
Why not?

LEN
Because if everything exists in accordance with your will there's no point in us trying to change it, is there? So there's no point in praying.

GOD

Is that what you think prayer means, trying to get me to change my mind?

LEN

Well, no, it's not the *whole* of prayer. I mean we can praise you and thank you as well. But I've always thought an important part of prayer was asking you for things.

GOD

You're quite right. That *is* an important part of prayer.

LEN

Then surely that must mean we can get you to change your mind.

GOD

Why?

LEN

Well, supposing I want a sunny day for an outing and I pray for a sunny day and I get a sunny day, surely I've persuaded you to change whatever plans you had for the weather on that day.

GOD

What makes you think my plans for the weather on that day were any other than a sunny day?

LEN

But if it was going to be a sunny day anyway, you haven't answered my prayer.

GOD

Haven't I? You prayed for a sunny day and you *got* a sunny day.

LEN

But not in answer to my prayer because it was going to be a sunny day anyway.

GOD

It was going to be a sunny day anyway in answer to your prayer.

LEN

I don't get that.

GOD
Let me put it this way. I am the source of everything that is, so everything in creation arises from my will, agreed?

LEN
Agreed.

GOD
Now, your prayer is part of creation, is it not?

LEN
Yes.

GOD
So your prayer arises from my will.

LEN
I suppose it does.

GOD
Do you see what that means?

LEN
Does it mean that you are responsible both for my prayer and for the sunny day?

GOD
It does.

LEN
But how can a sunny day be the answer to my prayer if you've already decided it's going to be a sunny day before I make the prayer?

GOD
Len, you are forgetting that I am not subject to time as you are. I exist outside time, remember? To put it in your terms, I decree what I decree from all eternity. So if I decree from all eternity that it is going to be a sunny day in answer to your prayer, then it will be a sunny day in answer to your prayer.

LEN
But if you decree it from all eternity surely my prayer has no bearing on the matter?

GOD
Certainly your prayer has not *forced* me to bring about the sunny day. But remember, I bring everything into existence. That means I arrange the whole pattern of cause and effect within creation.

LEN
How do you mean?

GOD
I mean I don't only bring about what happens in the universe, I also bring about what *causes* things to happen. For example, I cause the sun to give light and warmth to the earth. If you were to say, "God gives us light and warmth," you would be right, for I am the source of everything. But normally you would say, "The sun gives us light and warmth." And that is correct, too. I give you light and warmth by causing the sun to give you light and warmth.

LEN
Yes, I understand that, but where does prayer come in?

GOD
I'm coming to that, Len. Some of the things that happen in the universe are caused by people. For example, you planted some daffodil bulbs at the bottom of your garden and in the spring a lovely display of daffodils came up.

LEN
You noticed!

GOD
Of course I noticed. They are part of my creation, how could I *not* notice?

LEN
Oh, yes. Silly of me. But I was rather proud of them.

GOD
And you were quite right to be. They were beautiful.

LEN
But *you* created them, not *me*.

GOD

I know. But you planted them. You caused them to grow in that place at that time. I brought the daffodils into existence and caused them to grow, but they would not have grown at the bottom of your garden in the spring if you hadn't planted them there. In other words, just as – through me – the sun gives light and warmth to the earth, so – through me – those daffodils grew because you planted them.

LEN

So, in one way, I *did* cause them to grow?

GOD

Yes, you did.

LEN

I see.

GOD

Now, when you planted those bulbs, did you think you were interfering with my act of creation?

LEN

No. I was co-operating with your act of creation.

GOD
Right. It was my will that those daffodils should grow at the bottom of your garden, but it was also my will that they should grow at the bottom of your garden because you planted them there. Your planting them was part of the pattern of cause and effect which I decree from all eternity.

LEN
I'm beginning to see what you're driving at. Are you saying that prayer is answered in the same way?

GOD
Yes, I am. Can you see how?

LEN
I think so. Just as you intend some things in creation to be brought about through the *actions* of human beings, so you intend other things to be brought about through the *prayers* of human beings.

GOD
I couldn't have put it better myself.

LEN
So when we pray we're not trying to get you to change your mind?

GOD
No, you're not. You *can't* get me to change my mind. I can't change in any way at all. What I decree I decree from all eternity. But I decree that some things should be brought about through prayer, so when you pray you are asking me for those things.

LEN
But how do we know what those things are?

GOD
Why do you need to know?

LEN
Because there'd be no point in praying for them otherwise.

GOD
Really? When you planted those daffodil bulbs, did you know for certain they would all come up?

LEN

No, of course not. As a matter of fact, a couple of them failed to come up.

GOD

So even though you did not know for certain they would all come up, you didn't think it was a waste of time to plant them?

LEN

No.

GOD

Then why do you think it is a waste of time to pray if you do not know for certain whether I have decreed that such and such a thing should be brought about through prayer? Or, to put it another way, why do you think it is a waste of time to pray if you are not certain whether your prayer will be answered? Do you think you should only pray for things that are certain to be granted?

LEN

No. I suppose not.

GOD

You see, praying is necessary for some things to be brought about just as planting daffodil bulbs is necessary for some daffodils to come up.

LEN

So we don't change your mind or put pressure on you when we pray?

GOD

No, not in the least. Any more than planting a daffodil bulb puts pressure on me to create a daffodil.

LEN

You don't mind us asking for things in prayer, then?

GOD

Mind? Why should I mind?

LEN

Well, some people say it's superstitious to pray for things.

GOD

It *would* be superstitious if you thought I was a great magician in the sky who you could shout up to and try to persuade to give you things. But I hope I've shown you I'm not in the least like that.

LEN

But isn't it selfish to ask for things?

GOD

Not if the things you ask for are for your genuine good or for the good of others. In any case, I'd much rather you prayed for what you *really* wanted than for things you thought you *ought* to want.

LEN

But supposing the things I want are very trivial?

GOD

I love answering trivial prayers.

LEN

You do?

GOD

Oh yes. It's great fun.

LEN

But shouldn't we be more concerned with praising you and thanking you than with making trivial requests?

GOD
I don't mind really. If you ask for things, even trivial things, it means you recognise that I am the source of everything that is good – from marmalade butties to the air you breathe. It also means you realise that I am not a remote and distant figure, but someone close and familiar who wants the very best for you in every part of your life – from the sublime to the ridiculous. I think it's very important you should understand that, so asking for what you want when you pray is fine by me.

LEN
It's not an inferior form of prayer?

GOD
Not in the least. It's fundamental.

LEN
But if it is such an important and fundamental part of prayer, and a kind of prayer that you want us to pray, why is it so much of our prayer goes unanswered?

GOD
As I told you earlier, Len, my eternal purposes are beyond your understanding, so I cannot give you a full answer to that question. But I can suggest some ways you can think about what you call "unanswered" prayer.

LEN
Anything would be a help.

GOD
First of all, it can be useful to think of the way human beings grant or refuse requests to one another. For example, if a friend of yours asked you to make up a four for a game of golf on Saturday afternoon, and on the same Saturday afternoon your wife, Pat, asked you to take her shopping you would have to turn one of them down. Right?

LEN
Right.

GOD
In the same way if the farmer prays for rain and the vicar prays for fine weather for the garden fête I've got to turn one of them down. Right?

LEN
But you're all-powerful.

GOD
Come on, Len, we've already been through all that. I can't bring about a contradiction, remember?

LEN
I remember, I remember.

GOD
Fine. Now another example. Sometimes someone may ask you for something and, although you could grant their request, you have a very good reason for turning them down. For example, if a six-year-old asked you for the loan of a chisel, you'd probably refuse; not because you *couldn't* give it to them, but because it would be *dangerous* to give it to them. In a similar way I sometimes have good reasons for failing to answer a prayer.

LEN
Because what the person asked for wouldn't be good for them?

GOD
Sometimes that; but sometimes for other good reasons.

LEN
I see.

GOD
Then again, supposing a child asks his parents for a bike for his birthday because he can't think of anything that would make him happier. But his parents can't afford a bike. Instead they go out of their way to give him the most fabulous birthday ever. At the end of the day the boy might well say that it's been the happiest day of his life. His specific request has not been granted, but he has experienced the happiness he thought only a bike would bring. So, sometimes someone may pray for something and they do not get specifically what they asked for. But I may still have answered their prayer in some way.

LEN
You mean what they wanted may come about, but not in the way they wanted it?

GOD
Yes. What's important to realise, Len, is that no prayer is ever wasted. Even if it does not appear to you to be answered, it is never wasted. You see, although I want you to ask for things when you pray, that is not what prayer is really about.

LEN
Isn't it?

GOD
No. Up to now we've been talking as though prayer is about a creature asking me, the creator, to bring about certain things. But you've got to remember what I said earlier about sharing my divine life with you. The truth is that, when you pray, your primary relationship to me is not that of a creature to his creator but that of a child to his Father. When you pray you are drawn into communion with Jesus, my Son, and share in his relationship with me. That's why Jesus said, "Whatever you ask in my name…"

LEN
But if, when I pray, I am drawn into your own divine life, doesn't that mean that *you* play the important part, not me?

GOD
Yes, it does, Len. Prayer is *my* initiative, not yours. Prayer is the work of grace in you, the work of the Spirit in you. Prayer does not mean *you* trying to put pressure on *me*, or trying to change my mind; prayer means *me* doing something for *you*, drawing you deeper into my divine life of love.

LEN
So, asking for things in prayer is not important?

GOD
That's not what I said. I can use your needs, and wants, and anxieties and worries to draw you deeper into my life. You have to start where you *are*, Len, and where you *are* might be crying out for

what you want. I'll settle for that, I assure you. I can build on that. I will lead you, gradually, to understand where your true needs really lie and what your true wants really are.

LEN
And then what?

GOD
Then you will begin to understand that prayer is not primarily concerned with getting anything done, but is like lovers mooning about together, simply enjoying and delighting in each other's company.

FOR THOUGHT AND DISCUSSION

■ If prayers are not answered is there any point in praying?

■ Is there anything you cannot ask for in prayer?

■ How would you reply to someone who said, "My prayers haven't been answered, therefore there is no God"?

■ Is it selfish to pray for things for yourself?

■ Is it superstitious to ask for things in prayer?

■ Is prayer only for asking favours from God?

■ Prayer is a relationship. True or false?

Part Eight

A final message.

GOD
Why are you smiling?

LEN
I was just thinking back to the beginning of this dream.

GOD
And?

LEN
I was very much in awe of you when we first started talking.

GOD
Yes, you were, weren't you? A bit scared to ask me any questions, if I recall?

LEN
I was.

GOD
You seemed to lose your inhibitions, though, as time went on.

LEN
You made it easy for me.

GOD
Well, I tried my best.

LEN
You're quite nice, really, aren't you?

GOD
Thanks, Len.

LEN
That's OK. I'll feel a bit more relaxed when I pray to you in the future.

GOD
Good.

LEN
What's that funny noise?

GOD
It's your alarm-clock, Len.

LEN
What?

GOD
Your alarm-clock. Time to get up.

LEN
Oh, no, it can't be! There's lots more I want to ask you.

GOD
Another time, Len. You've got quite enough to think about for the moment.

LEN
That noise! It's getting louder.

GOD
Just your alarm-clock.

LEN
And your voice is getting fainter.

GOD
You're waking up, Len.

LEN
But I don't want to.

GOD
Never mind. You'll dream of me again sometime.

LEN
But I don't want you to leave me.

GOD
Leave you? How can you imagine that I'll leave you after all we've been talking about? I'm closer to you than you are to yourself. Always.

LEN
Yes, so you are. I was forgetting. But how do I keep in touch with you?

GOD
Look inwards, Len; look into yourself. You'll always find me there.

LEN
Thanks. I'll do that. But before I wake up can't you just tell me how to lead my life? Give me some advice? Tell me what you want me to do?

GOD
You're doing all right, Len. You don't need any further directions from me.

LEN
At least give me something to remember.

GOD
There's only one thing you need to remember.

LEN
What's that?

GOD
It's all about love.

LEN
What is?

GOD
My life; your life. The whole universe. It's all about love.

LEN
All about love. I'll remember.

GOD
And Len?

LEN
Yes?

GOD
I love you.

LEN
What? The noise is getting louder. I can't hear you.

GOD
I said, I love you, Len. I love you, Len. I love you, Len…

LEN
The noise, the noise…

In the semi-darkness Len gropes for the alarm-clock. He finds it and switches it off. Silence. Half-asleep, he fancies he can still hear the words:

I love you, Len. I love you, Len. I love you, Len.

Slowly he comes to full consciousness. His wife, Pat, is leaning over him and whispering in his ear.

PAT
I love you, Len. I love you, Len. I love you, Len.

LEN
Oh…what a nice way to wake up.

PAT
I thought you might like it.

LEN
Love! Love! Love! That's what it's all about, you know.

PAT
What *what's* all about?

LEN
Everything.